Guide to Eclipse X

Practical Guide

V. Telman

Practical Guide

1.Introduction

Eclipse X is a next-generation Integrated Development Environment (IDE) developed as an evolution of the renowned Eclipse platform. Born as an open-source project, Eclipse X represents a significant leap forward in functionality, performance, and flexibility compared to its predecessors, catering to software developers working in various programming languages and on multiple platforms. This IDE is highly modular, featuring a robust plugin infrastructure that allows customization of the environment based on the specific needs of a project or development team.

One of the core features of Eclipse X is its support for multi-language projects, with advanced integrations for languages such as Java, C++, Python, JavaScript, and more. Thanks to its plugin-based architecture, Eclipse X can expand its functionalities with additional modules, making it extremely flexible and suitable for a wide range of software projects, from building simple web applications to complex embedded systems or cloud-native applications.

Key Features of Eclipse X

1. **Modularity and Plugins**

Eclipse X is built around a modular architecture that allows users to add or remove functionalities through specific plugins. This makes it a customizable environment tailored to user needs. For instance, if you are a Java developer, you can install the Java Development Tools (JDT), while for web development, you can integrate plugins like the Web Tools Platform (WTP).

2. **Multi-language Development Support**

Unlike other IDEs, Eclipse X provides native support for various programming languages, including Java, C++, Python, and even scripting languages like JavaScript. Thanks to its plugin platform, each language has its own specific set of tools, including dedicated editors, code completion suggestions, and integrations with build and versioning systems.

3. **Git and DevOps Integration**

Eclipse X offers advanced integration with Git, providing graphical tools for version control management directly from the IDE interface. Additionally, through a series of DevOps plugins, it is possible to integrate Eclipse X with Continuous Integration/Continuous Deployment (CI/CD) pipelines like Jenkins, Docker, and Kubernetes.

4. **Advanced Debugger**

Eclipse X provides powerful debugging tools that support the debugging of multi-threaded and distributed applications. You can set breakpoints, step through code, analyze variable states, and inspect memory in real time.

5. **Improved and Flexible UI**

The user interface of Eclipse X has been redesigned to be more intuitive and responsive, with a modern design that offers greater flexibility in managing windows and workspaces. Users can now customize the interface according to their preferences, moving panels and reorganizing tools as needed.

6. **Cloud-native Development Support**

Eclipse X is optimized for developing cloud-native applications, with integrations for Kubernetes and Docker. With these features, developers can manage containers directly from the IDE and deploy applications to cloud-based production environments with ease.

Recognizing the Features of Eclipse X

When using Eclipse X, you may encounter a variety of features that can make a difference in the development cycle. Below are some key functionalities that set Eclipse X apart:

1. **Code Highlighting and Advanced Auto-completion**

Eclipse X employs powerful syntax highlighting mechanisms to help developers quickly identify syntax errors or logical issues in the code. The auto-completion is highly advanced, even supporting contextual suggestions based on static code analysis.

2. **Code Control and Refactoring**

One of the most powerful tools in Eclipse X is automatic refactoring, which allows for quick and safe restructuring of code. Features like renaming variables or classes, code modularization, and automatic reindenting help keep the code clean and readable.

3. **Automated Build and Project

Management**

Eclipse X supports automated build management through tools like Maven and Gradle. You can easily configure build pipelines, run unit tests, and deploy your application directly from the IDE.

4. **Dependency and Development Environment Management**

Through integration with dependency management systems like Maven, Eclipse X allows easy management of the packages and libraries needed for your project. Moreover, the virtual environment management system enables you to run projects in isolated environments, avoiding dependency conflicts.

System Requirements

To install and use Eclipse X efficiently, certain system requirements must be met. Below are the minimum and recommended requirements:

Minimum Requirements:

- **Operating System**: Windows 10/11, macOS 10.15 or later, Ubuntu 20.04+ or other Linux distributions.

- **Processor**: Dual-core CPU of at least 2.0 GHz.

- **RAM**: 4 GB of RAM.

- **Disk Space**: At least 2 GB of free space for installation.

- **Java Runtime Environment (JRE)**: JRE 11 or higher.

- **Internet Connection**: Required for downloading and updating plugins.

Recommended Requirements:

- **Processor**: Quad-core CPU of 2.5 GHz or higher.

- **RAM**: 8 GB or more to handle complex projects.

- **Disk Space**: 10 GB or more for large

projects, including additional plugins.

- **Graphics Card**: Graphics card with OpenGL 3.2 support for advanced visualization features.

Installing Eclipse X

The installation of Eclipse X is a simple and intuitive process, varying slightly depending on the operating system in use. Here is a step-by-step guide for installing Eclipse X:

1. **Download the Installation Package**

The first step to install Eclipse X is to visit the official project site (www.eclipse.org) and download the correct version for your operating system. Eclipse X is available for Windows, macOS, and Linux.

2. **Installation on Windows**

- After downloading the installer for Windows, run the `.exe` file.

- Select the installation path and accept the terms and conditions.

- The installer will propose a list of preconfigured development environments (e.g., Java, C++, Web Development). Choose the desired one or customize the installation.

- Once the installation is complete, launch Eclipse X from the Start menu or desktop shortcut.

3. **Installation on macOS**

- Download the `.dmg` file from the official site.

- Mount the disk image and drag the Eclipse X icon into the **Applications** folder.

- Launch Eclipse X from the **Launchpad** or the **Applications** folder.

- On macOS, you may need to grant additional permissions to allow the program to run, as it is not downloaded from the App Store.

4. **Installation on Linux**

- Download the `.tar.gz` file from the Eclipse website.

- Open a terminal and decompress the package with the command:

```bash
tar -xzvf eclipse-x.tar.gz
```

- Move the decompressed folder to `/opt/` or another system directory with the following command:

```bash
sudo mv eclipse-x /opt/
```

- Create a shortcut in the applications menu:

```bash
sudo ln -s /opt/eclipse-x/eclipse /usr/bin/eclipse-x
```

- Start Eclipse X by typing `eclipse-x` in the terminal.

5. **First Run and Configuration**

Upon the first launch of Eclipse X, you will be prompted to select a workspace directory. This is the folder where your projects will be saved. You can use the default folder or choose a custom one. Additionally, Eclipse X will check for updates for installed plugins and the IDE itself.

User Interface

Overview of the GUI

The graphical user interface (GUI) of Eclipse X has been designed to be highly modular and adaptable to developers' needs. The basic structure consists of various "perspectives," each optimized for a specific type of development activity (e.g., Java, debugging, Git). Each perspective contains windows (or **views**) that display different information or tools, such as the code editor, project navigator, and console.

1. **Main Menu**

The main menu is located at the top of the application window and includes standard entries such as **File**, **Edit**, **Navigate**, **Project**, **Run**, **Window**, and **Help**. From here, you can access the main functionalities of Eclipse X, including project management, plugin installation, and IDE configuration.

2. **Toolbar**

Below the main menu is the **toolbar**, a bar of tools with icons for quickly performing frequent operations, such as saving a file, running a program, or starting the debugger.

3. **Perspectives and Layout**

The central part of the interface is reserved for the main workspace area, which changes depending on the selected perspective. For example:

- **Java Perspective**: includes a code editor, a package navigation window, and a console for displaying program output.

- **Debug Perspective**: offers debugging tools, such as variable views and breakpoints.

Perspectives can be customized by adding or removing views based on needs.

4. **Code Editor**

The code editor is the central component of Eclipse X. It supports advanced features like syntax highlighting, auto-completion, code navigation (e.g., jumping directly to a function declaration), and code refactoring.

5. **Console and Output**

At the bottom of the window is the **console**, which shows the output of the executed program or errors detected during compilation.

Customizing the Interface

Eclipse X allows for a high degree of customization of the GUI to suit personal preferences and project needs. For example, you can:

- **Modify Window Layout**: Drag and drop windows to position them in different areas of the screen.

- **Change Themes and Colors**: Through the IDE settings, you can choose between default themes like **light** or **dark**, and modify the editor's colors for better readability and contrast.

- **Manage Perspectives**: Create custom perspectives with specific views for certain activities, such as one for Java development and another for debugging.

Navigating the Work Environment

Effectively navigating the Eclipse X work environment is essential for productive work. Some key techniques for navigating the project include:

- **Navigating Between Files and Classes**

: Using the **Ctrl+Shift+R** (Windows/Linux) or **Cmd+Shift+R** (macOS) command, you can quickly open files within the project.

- **Quick Code Jumps**: **Ctrl+Click** on a variable or function allows you to jump to the corresponding declaration.

- **Advanced Searches**: Eclipse X includes powerful search tools, such as global search within the project or filtering by file type.

Moreover, the IDE supports navigation through keyboard shortcuts, significantly simplifying interaction for experienced users.

2.Creating Projects in Eclipse X

Eclipse X is a powerful integrated development environment (IDE) that allows you to manage complex programming projects through a clear and modular structure. Effective project management in Eclipse X is essential for software development, as it helps organize code, resources, libraries, and dependencies, making collaboration among development teams easier and facilitating the software lifecycle management. In this guide, we will explore in detail how to start a new project, import and export existing projects, and the structure of projects in Eclipse X, with practical examples.

Starting a New Project in Eclipse X

1. Selecting the Project Type

Creating a new project in Eclipse X is simple and flexible. First, you need to select the type of project to create. Depending on the programming language and the nature of the project, Eclipse X offers various predefined templates, such as Java, C++, Web (HTML/CSS/JavaScript), Python, and more. These templates include initial configurations that facilitate project management.

Example: Creating a Java Project

To start a new Java project in Eclipse X, follow these steps:

1. **File -> New -> Project**: In the main menu, click on **File**, then select **New** and finally **Project**.

2. **Select Project Type**: In the dialog that opens, you will find a list of available project types. Select **Java** and then **Java Project**. If you are working with a different language, select the corresponding project type (e.g., **Web Project** for HTML or

C++ Project for C++).

3. **Project Name**: Enter a meaningful name for the project, such as "CustomerManagement." This name will represent the main folder where all the code and resources will be organized.

4. **Project Location**: You can use the default location (the default workspace) or specify a different folder where you want to save the project.

5. **Runtime Configuration**: If the project requires a specific version of Java or a JDK, you can configure it here. Eclipse X will try to automatically set the correct version, but you can always specify a different one.

6. **Finalize**: Once you have configured the options, click **Finish** to create the project.

At this point, Eclipse X will automatically

create the basic structure of the project, including folders like **src** (for source code) and **bin** (for compiled files).

2. Configuring a Custom Project Environment

For more complex projects, Eclipse X offers the possibility to configure a custom environment. After creating the project, you can access the project settings by right-clicking on the project name in the **Package Explorer** and selecting **Properties**.

Some common options include:

- **Libraries**: In this section, you can add external libraries, such as JAR files, needed for the project.
- **Compilation**: You can configure the compiler version, error and warning behaviors, and other compilation options.

- **Runtime Environment**: Configuration of the JRE or other specific project dependencies.

- **Build Path**: This option allows you to manage the project's build path, including adding external paths for libraries or modules.

Example: Adding an External Library (JAR)

Suppose you want to add an external library, such as **Apache Commons** for string operations. Follow these steps:

1. **Right-click on Project -> Properties -> Java Build Path**.

2. **Select "Libraries" -> Add External JARs**.

3. **Navigate to the JAR**: Select the JAR

file of the library you downloaded on your computer (e.g., `commons-lang3-3.12.0.jar`).

4. **Confirm and Apply**: After adding the JAR, click **Apply and Close**.

Now, your project can utilize the features of the external library.

3. Adding Modules or Dependencies

If your project has multiple modules or dependencies, you can easily add them through Eclipse X's project management system. For example, if you are using Maven or Gradle to manage your Java project's dependencies, Eclipse X offers native integration with these tools.

Example: Adding a Dependency with Maven

1. **Right-click on Project -> Configure -> Convert to Maven Project**.

2. **Pom.xml**: After converting the project to a Maven project, Eclipse X will generate a `pom.xml` file in the project's root.

3. **Add Dependencies**: Modify the `pom.xml` file to include the necessary dependencies. For example, to add the Apache Commons Lang dependency:

```xml
<dependency>

<groupId>org.apache.commons</groupId>
    <artifactId>commons-lang3</artifactId>
    <version>3.12.0</version>
</dependency>
```

4. **Save and Update**: Once you save the file, Eclipse X will automatically download the dependency from the central Maven repository.

Importing and Exporting Projects

One of the most useful features of Eclipse X is the ability to easily import and export projects to and from other machines or repositories. This functionality is essential for collaboration in development teams, especially when using a version control system like Git.

1. Importing a Project into Eclipse X

Eclipse X offers several ways to import a project, whether it is an existing Eclipse project, a Maven project, a Gradle project, or even projects from a Git repository.

Example: Importing an Existing Eclipse Project

If you have an Eclipse project saved locally or on an external storage device, you can import it by following these steps:

1. **File -> Import -> Existing Projects into Workspace**.

2. **Select Project Folder**: In the dialog that appears, select the **Existing Projects** option and click **Browse** to find the folder containing the project you want to import.

3. **Select the Project**: Once the correct folder is selected, Eclipse X will list the available projects within that directory. Select

the project or projects you want to import.

4. **Finish**: Click **Finish** to complete the import. Eclipse X will add the project to your workspace and it will be ready for modification or execution.

Example: Importing a Project from a Git Repository

If you want to import a project from a Git repository, Eclipse X has full integration with Git, making this process very simple.

1. **File -> Import -> Git -> Projects from Git**.

2. **Clone URI**: In the dialog, select **Clone URI**. You will need to enter the URL of the Git repository you want to clone (for example, `https://github.com/user/project.git`).

3. **Authentication**: If the repository is private, you will need to enter your username and password (or access token) to authenticate.

4. **Select the Branch**: Choose which branch of the project you want to clone (for example, `main` or `develop`).

5. **Import into Workspace**: Eclipse X will ask if you want to import the project directly into the workspace as an existing project. Select this option and proceed with the import.

2. Exporting a Project

Exporting a project is useful when you need to share your work with other developers or when you want to archive the project in a format usable on other machines. There are several export options in Eclipse X, depending on your needs.

Example: Exporting a Java Project to a JAR File

To distribute a Java library or application, it is often useful to export the project to a JAR file. Here are the steps to do this:

1. **File -> Export -> Java -> JAR File**.

2. **Select the Project**: In the dialog, select the project or files you want to include in the JAR file.

3. **Specify the Destination**: Choose a location on the disk to save the exported JAR file and enter a name for the file, such as `CustomerManagement.jar`.

4. **Export Options**: You can select additional options, such as including resources

or external libraries in the JAR file.

5. **Conclusion**: Click **Finish** to complete the export. Eclipse X will generate the JAR file, ready to be used as a library or executable application.

Example: Exporting a Project as a ZIP Archive

If you want to share the project with another developer using Eclipse, you can export it as a ZIP archive. This includes all the source code, resources, and project configurations.

1. **File -> Export -> General Archive File -> ZIP Archive**.

2. **Select the Project**: In the dialog, select the project you want to export.

3. **Specify the Destination**: Choose the location to save the ZIP archive and enter a name for the file (e.g., `CustomerManagementProject.zip`).

4. **Conclusion**: Click **Finish** to complete the export. You can now share the ZIP file with other developers, who can easily import it into Eclipse X.

Project Structure in Eclipse X

The structure of a project in Eclipse X is a fundamental aspect of organizing code and resources in a clear and accessible manner. Depending on the type of project, the structure may vary, but the typical configuration of a Java project, for example, includes the following folders and files:

1. `src` Folder (Source Code)

The `src` folder is the main directory where the source code is stored. Each source file (e.g., `.java` files for Java projects) is organized within packages. Packages represent a logical division of the project and follow a hierarchical naming convention (e.g., `com.company.project.module`).

Example:

```

CustomerManagement/

├── src/

│   └── com/

│       └── company/

│           └── customers/

│               ├── Main.java

│               ├── Customer.java

│               └── CustomerManagement.java
```

``

`

In this example, the `Main.java` class contains the `main` method, the entry point of the application, while `Customer.java` and `CustomerManagement.java` are other classes implementing the project's functionalities.

2. `bin` Folder (Compiled Files)

The `bin` folder contains the compiled files from the project. When compiling a Java project, for example, `.java` files are converted into `.class` files, which are executable by the Java Virtual Machine (JVM). This folder is managed automatically by Eclipse and should not be modified manually.

3. `lib` Folder (Libraries)

If the project uses external libraries, these can be placed in the `lib` folder. JAR files or other external libraries are included in this folder to be linked to the project.

Example:

```
CustomerManagement/
├── lib/
│   ├── commons-lang3-3.12.0.jar
│   └── gson-2.8.8.jar
```

In this case, the project uses two external libraries: **Apache Commons Lang** and **Gson**.

4. Project Configuration Files

Every Eclipse project includes configuration files that describe the settings and properties of the project. Some of the most common files are:

- `.classpath`: Defines the build path, including references to external libraries and resources.

- `.project`: Contains general information about the project, such as the name and basic settings.

- `pom.xml` or `build.gradle`: If the project uses Maven or Gradle, these files manage dependencies and build configurations.

Example of `.classpath` file:

```xml
<classpath>
  <classpathentry kind="src" path="src"/>
  <classpathentry kind="con" path="org.eclipse.jdt.launching.JRE_CONTAINER"/>
```

```
  <classpathentry kind="lib"
path="lib/commons-lang3-3.12.0.jar"/>
  <classpathentry kind="output" path="bin"/>
</classpath>
```

This file indicates that the source code is located in the `src` folder, that it uses the external library `commons-lang3`, and that the compiled files are saved in the `bin` folder.

5. Additional Folders (Resources, Tests, etc.)

More complex projects may include other folders, such as:

- **resources**: for images, configuration files, or other assets.
- **test**: for unit or integration tests (e.g., `src/test/java`).

3.Using the Editor and Tools in Eclipse X

Eclipse X is a versatile and powerful IDE that provides an integrated development environment with advanced features for writing, debugging, and managing source code. The IDE supports numerous programming languages and offers customizable tools that enhance the development experience. This guide provides a detailed overview of using the **source code editor**, **advanced editor features**, and **debugging tools** in Eclipse X, with practical examples to help maximize your productivity.

Source Code Editor

The source code editor in Eclipse X is the core of the IDE and supports a wide range of languages, including Java, C++, Python, JavaScript, and many others. In addition to basic features like syntax highlighting, the editor provides advanced tools for code completion, code navigation, library management, and much more.

1. Editor Interface

When you open a source code file in Eclipse X, it is displayed in the **code editor** at the center of the interface. The editor is designed to be intuitive and productive, offering various tools directly accessible while you write code. Below are the main components of the editor:

- **Line Numbers**: On the left, you can see the line numbers, useful for debugging and navigation.

- **Syntax Highlighting**: The editor highlights keywords, comments, strings, and other code elements in different colors to improve readability.

- **Status Bar**: Shows useful information about the currently open file, such as the number of lines, cursor position, and file type.

- **Code Completion**: Eclipse X offers

context-based code suggestions as you type, enhancing coding speed and accuracy.

Example: Opening and Editing a Java File

Imagine you are working on a Java project and want to open and edit a class named `CustomerManagement.java`. Follow these steps:

1. **Open the Class**: Go to the **Package Explorer** (on the left side of the window), expand the package containing the Java file, and double-click on `CustomerManagement.java`.

2. **Editing the Code**: You can now start modifying the code directly in the editor. For example, if you want to add a new method to the class:

   ```java
   ```

```
public void addCustomer(String firstName, String lastName) {
    Customer customer = new Customer(firstName, lastName);
    customers.add(customer);
}
```

You will notice that Eclipse X highlights the syntax with different colors for keywords like `public`, data types like `String`, and variable names like `customer`.

3. **Code Completion**: While typing, Eclipse X will automatically suggest existing methods and variables. For instance, if you start typing `customers.`, a list of available methods or attributes for the `customers` object will be suggested, reducing the time needed to write code and minimizing errors.

2. Syntax Highlighting and Customization

Syntax highlighting is one of the most important features of the source code editor. Different programming languages have specific color schemes to facilitate code reading and error detection.

Example: Customizing Highlighting Colors

If you want to customize the highlighting colors in the editor, you can do so through the settings:

1. **Go to Window -> Preferences -> General -> Appearance -> Colors and Fonts**.

2. **Code Editor**: Select the **Code Editor** option and customize the colors for elements like comments, strings, keywords, and numbers. You can choose a predefined scheme or create a custom one.

3. Other Basic Editor Features

The source code editor in Eclipse X also includes several other useful features:

- **Automatic Code Formatting**: Eclipse X can automatically format the code according to the guidelines of the programming language you are using. You can format the code by selecting **Source -> Format** or using the keyboard shortcut **Ctrl+Shift+F**.

- **Refactoring**: Refactoring tools allow you to safely rename variables, methods, or classes while automatically updating all corresponding instances in the code.

- **Code Navigation**: You can easily navigate the code by holding **Ctrl+Click** on a method or variable, which will take you to its declaration. For example, by **Ctrl+Clicking** on `customer` in the method above, Eclipse X will take you to the declaration of the `Customer` class.

Advanced Editor Features

In addition to basic features, the Eclipse X editor offers advanced tools that help streamline the development process and improve code quality. These tools include intelligent code completion, advanced refactoring, and integration with version control systems like Git.

1. Code Completion and Contextual Suggestions

One of the most powerful features of Eclipse X is **automatic code completion**. This feature not only suggests methods, variables, and classes but also takes into account the context you are working in, providing more precise suggestions.

Example: Completing Methods in a Java Class

Suppose you have a `Customer` class with the following methods:

```java
public class Customer {
  private String firstName;
  private String lastName;

  public String getFirstName() {
     return firstName;
  }

  public String getLastName() {
     return lastName;
  }
}
```

```

Now, if in another class you start typing:

```java
Customer customer = new Customer();

customer.get
```

Eclipse X will automatically suggest the available methods `getFirstName()` and `getLastName()` from the `Customer` class, allowing you to quickly choose the correct method. This feature not only speeds up development but also reduces errors.

2. Code Refactoring

Refactoring is a key process for keeping code clean and maintainable, and Eclipse X
```

provides robust tools to perform this operation. Some of the main refactoring operations include:

- **Rename**: Safely change the names of variables, methods, or classes throughout the project.

- **Extract Method**: Create new methods from selected portions of code to improve modularity.

- **Change Method Signature**: Change the parameters or return type of a method without manually updating all method calls.

Example: Safe Renaming of a Variable

Suppose you want to rename a variable `customerName` to `userName` throughout the project. Here's how to do it:

1. **Select the Variable**: Select `customerName` in the editor.

2. **Right-click -> Refactor -> Rename** or use **Alt+Shift+R**: A text field will open, allowing you to enter the new name.

3. **Enter the New Name**: Type `userName` and press **Enter**. Eclipse X will automatically update all instances of `customerName` in the project.

3. Code Inspection and Correction

Eclipse X provides code inspection tools that detect errors, warnings, and potential improvements while you write. Warnings are displayed as **underlines** or **error icons** to the left of the line of code.

Example: Automatic Error Correction

If you forget to import a library, Eclipse X

will display a warning. For example, if you use `List` without importing the corresponding class, Eclipse X will show an error and automatically suggest importing `java.util.List`.

1. **Select the Fix**: Click on the small icon with a light bulb or press **Ctrl+1**.

2. **Suggestion**: Eclipse X will suggest importing `java.util.List`.

Select the option, and the import will be automatically added at the top of the file.

Debugging Tools

Debugging is a crucial part of software development, and Eclipse X provides a comprehensive set of tools for identifying and fixing bugs in the code. These tools allow you to execute code step-by-step, examine variables in real time, and monitor the program flow.

1. Adding Breakpoints

A **breakpoint** is a bookmark that pauses the program's execution at a specific point, allowing you to examine the state of variables and the code execution.

Example: Setting a Breakpoint in a Java Method

Suppose you have the following method in `CustomerManagement.java`:

```java
public void addCustomer(String firstName,
```

```
String lastName) {

  Customer customer = new
Customer(firstName, lastName);

  customers.add(customer);

}
```

To debug, you can add a breakpoint on the line that creates a new `Customer` object:

1. **Add the Breakpoint**: Click on the left bar next to the line `Customer customer = new Customer(firstName, lastName);`. A small blue circle will appear, indicating that a breakpoint has been set.

2. **Start Debugging**: Go to **Run -> Debug** or press **F11** to run the program in debug mode. When the program reaches the breakpoint, it will stop.

2. Step-Through Execution

Once the program is paused at the breakpoint, you can execute it **step-by-step** to observe how variables change and how the program flow evolves.

- **Step Into (F5)**: Enter the current method to examine its internals.

- **Step Over (F6)**: Execute the current line and move to the next one without entering the methods.

- **Step Return (F7)**: Complete the execution of the current method and return to the caller.

3. Viewing Variables

During debugging, Eclipse X allows you to view and modify the values of variables in real time through the **Variables View**. This view displays all local and global variables with their respective values.

Example: Monitoring a Variable

Suppose the `addCustomer` method has an issue and you want to check the content of the `firstName` variable during execution. After setting a breakpoint, Eclipse X will halt execution and show the local variables in the **Variables** view. Here, you can inspect the value of `firstName` to see if it matches the expected value.

4. Exploring the Call Stack

The **Call Stack** displays the sequence of method calls that led to the current point in the program. This is particularly useful for understanding

where a method was called from and how you arrived at the breakpoint.

Eclipse X offers a wide range of tools for code development, from an advanced source code editor to powerful debugging tools. With features like intelligent code completion, code refactoring, real-time error analysis, and a complete set of debugging tools, Eclipse X supports developers at every stage of the software lifecycle, enhancing productivity and reducing the number of errors in the code.

By effectively using these tools, you can improve the quality of your code and significantly speed up the development process.

4.Supported Programming Languages in Eclipse X

Eclipse X is one of the most versatile and flexible integrated development environments (IDEs), known for its support of a wide range of programming languages. The core of Eclipse X is designed to be modular, allowing developers to configure custom development environments with plugins that add support for various languages and frameworks. From classic Java to modern languages like Python and JavaScript, Eclipse X offers robust support with advanced features for development, dependency management, and debugging.

In this guide, we will explore in detail the main **supported programming languages** in Eclipse X, the configuration of development environments for each, and some **practical usage examples**. We will cover languages such as **Java**, **Python**, **C/C++**, **JavaScript**, **PHP**, **Ruby**, and others, demonstrating how to set them up within Eclipse X and use them effectively.

Configuring Development Environments in Eclipse X

To configure a development environment in Eclipse X for a specific language, it is necessary to install the appropriate plugins that provide tools, libraries, and support for the chosen language. By default, Eclipse X is distributed with support for Java, but with a few steps, you can add environments for other programming languages.

1. Installing Plugins in Eclipse X

Eclipse X is highly extensible thanks to its plugin system. Most languages require a specific plugin that you can install directly from within the IDE.

Steps to Install a Plugin:

1. **Open Eclipse X** and go to the **Help -> Eclipse Marketplace** menu.

2. In the search bar, enter the name of the language or the plugin you wish to install, such as **Python**, **JavaScript**, **PHP**, or **C++**.

3. Find the appropriate plugin in the search results. For example, for Python, you would look for **PyDev**.

4. Click on **Install** and follow the instructions to complete the installation.

5. Once installed, Eclipse X may prompt you to restart the IDE.

After installing the plugin, Eclipse X will be configured to support the chosen language, allowing you to create new projects for that language.

2. Configuring the Development Environment for Java

Java is the primary language natively supported by Eclipse X. When you install Eclipse X, it comes with a default configuration for developing Java applications.

Steps to Configure a Java Project:

1. **Create a New Project**: Go to **File -> New -> Java Project**.

2. **Configure the Project**: Enter a name for the project, such as `ExampleJavaProject`.

3. **Specify the JRE**: Select the version of the **Java Runtime Environment (JRE)** you want to use for the project. Eclipse X is compatible with all major Java versions (Java 8, 11, 17, etc.).

4. **Project Structure**: After creating the project, Eclipse X will generate the basic structure with a `src` folder for source code.

5. **Write Code**: You can now add classes and write Java code.

Practical Example: Creating a Java Class

```java
public class HelloWorld {
    public static void main(String[] args) {
        System.out.println("Hello, world from Eclipse X!");
    }
}
```

To run the code, right-click on the class and select **Run As -> Java Application**.

3. Configuring the Development Environment for Python

To develop in **Python** in Eclipse X, one of the most popular plugins is **PyDev**, which provides full support for Python 2.x and 3.x, including tools for debugging, auto-completion, and dependency management.

Installing PyDev:

1. **Help -> Eclipse Marketplace**.

2. Search for **PyDev** and click **Install**.

3. After installation, restart Eclipse X.

Creating a Python Project:

1. **Create a New Python Project**: Go to **File -> New -> Python Project**.

2. **Specify the Python Interpreter**: If this is your first time configuring PyDev, you will need to specify the path to the Python interpreter (such as `python3`).

3. **Project Structure**: PyDev will organize the project by creating a `src` folder where you can write your Python code.

Practical Example: Creating a Python Script

```python
```

```
def greet():

    print("Hello, world from Python in Eclipse X!")


if __name__ == "__main__":

    greet()
```

To run the script, right-click on the file and select **Run As -> Python Application**.

4. Configuring the Development Environment for C/C++

Eclipse X also supports **C** and **C++** through the **CDT (C/C++ Development Tools)** plugin. This plugin provides a complete environment for C and C++ development, with features such as syntax highlighting, debugging, and compiler support.

Installing the CDT Plugin:

1. **Help -> Eclipse Marketplace**.

2. Search for **C/C++ Development Tools (CDT)** and click **Install**.

3. Restart Eclipse X after installation.

Creating a C/C++ Project:

1. **Create a New C/C++ Project**: Go to **File -> New -> C/C++ Project**.

2. **Select the Project Type**: Choose between a **C** or **C++** project and specify whether it is a simple command-line application or a more complex project.

3. **Specify the Compiler**: Ensure you have a compiler installed (such as GCC) and that it is correctly configured.

Practical Example: Creating a C Program

```c
```

```
#include <stdio.h>


int main() {
    printf("Hello, world from C in Eclipse X!\n");
    return 0;
}
```

To compile and run the program, right-click on the file and select **Run As -> C/C++ Application**.

5. Configuring the Development Environment for JavaScript

Eclipse X can also be used for **JavaScript** development, with plugins like **Wild Web Developer** that provide support for JavaScript, HTML, CSS, Node.js, and other web development tools.

Installing the Wild Web Developer Plugin:

1. **Help -> Eclipse Marketplace**.

2. Search for **Wild Web Developer** and click **Install**.

3. Restart Eclipse X after installation.

Creating a JavaScript Project:

1. **Create a New Web Project**: Go to **File -> New -> Web Project** and select **Static Web Project**.

2. **Write JavaScript Code**: You can create a new `.js` file within the project structure.

Practical Example: Creating a JavaScript File

```javascript

function greet() {

    console.log("Hello, world from JavaScript
```

in Eclipse X!");

}

greet();

```

You can run the JavaScript code directly in the browser or using **Node.js** if you have configured the Node environment in Eclipse X.

### 6. Configuring the Development Environment for PHP

Eclipse X can be configured to support the development of **PHP** applications via the **PHP Development Tools (PDT)** plugin, which provides features such as syntax highlighting, auto-completion, and debugging for PHP.
```

Installing the PDT Plugin:

1. **Help -> Eclipse Marketplace**.

2. Search for **PHP Development Tools (PDT)** and click **Install**.

3. Restart Eclipse X after installation.

Creating a PHP Project:

1. **Create a New PHP Project**: Go to **File -> New -> PHP Project**.

2. **Write PHP Code**: You can create `.php` files within the project.

Practical Example: Creating a PHP File

```php

<?php

function greet() {

    echo "Hello, world from PHP in Eclipse X!";

}
```

greet();

?>

```

You can run the PHP file on a local server like Apache or using tools like **XAMPP**.

### 7. Configuring the Development Environment for Ruby

**Ruby** is also supported in Eclipse X thanks to the **DLTK (Dynamic Languages Toolkit)** plugin, which offers tools for the development of dynamic languages such as Ruby, Perl, and Tcl.

#### Installing the DLTK Plugin:

1. **Help -> Eclipse Marketplace**.

2. Search for **Dynamic Languages Toolkit
```

(DLTK)** and click **Install**.

3. Restart Eclipse X after installation.

Creating a Ruby Project:

1. **Create a New Ruby Project**: Go to **File -> New -> Ruby Project**.

2. **Write Ruby Code**: You can create `.rb` files within the project.

Practical Example: Creating a Ruby Script

```ruby
def greet
  puts "Hello, world from Ruby in Eclipse X!"
end


greet
```

You can run the script directly in Eclipse X using **Run As -> Ruby Application**.

Eclipse X stands out for its ability to support a wide range of programming languages through the installation of dedicated plugins. This versatility makes it an extremely powerful development environment for various projects, from backend to frontend, and from desktop applications to websites. We have explored how to configure Eclipse X for languages like **Java**, **Python**, **C/C++**, **JavaScript**, **PHP**, and **Ruby**, demonstrating with practical examples how to start a project for each language.

Using Eclipse X as a multi-language IDE allows developers to efficiently manage different projects, optimizing the development and debugging processes in a single environment. This flexibility is one of the key strengths of Eclipse X, which continues to be a popular choice among professional developers worldwide.

5.Dependency Management in Eclipse X

Dependency management is a crucial aspect of modern software development, as applications increasingly rely on external libraries and frameworks. In Eclipse X, advanced tools like **Maven** and **Gradle** simplify dependency management by automating the inclusion of external packages, updating libraries, and managing versions. These tools are essential for large-scale projects, where keeping track of dependencies is vital for ensuring code stability and security.

In this guide, we will explore in detail:

- **Introduction to library management**: Why it's important and how Eclipse X supports it.

- **Configuring Maven and Gradle in Eclipse X**: How to set up and use these popular tools for dependency management.

- **Practical examples**: Configurations, dependency management, and using external repositories.

Introduction to Library Management

External libraries, or dependencies, are software components that a project can use to avoid rewriting existing code. They can include frameworks, third-party libraries, various utilities, and are distributed as precompiled packages. Manually managing these dependencies can become complex and error-prone, especially when using different versions or needing to resolve conflicts between libraries.

Why is Dependency Management Important?

1. **Time savings**: Including an existing library allows you to avoid rewriting code. For instance, you can use a library for database access, reducing the time needed to develop a solution from scratch.

2. **Version management**: Dependencies can be updated over time with new features or bug fixes. A dependency management system helps keep the project up to date.

3. **Conflict resolution**: In large projects, different libraries may require different versions of other dependencies. Management tools like Maven and Gradle help automatically resolve these conflicts.

How Eclipse X Manages Dependencies

Eclipse X can manage dependencies natively by integrating popular tools like **Maven** and **Gradle**. These tools offer significant advantages:

- **Automation**: Downloading and managing libraries happens automatically.

- **Version control**: You can specify exact versions of each library to use.

- **Support for remote repositories**: Libraries are automatically downloaded from remote repositories like Maven Central or custom company repositories.

- **Seamless integration with Eclipse X**: The IDE natively supports Maven and Gradle, making the configuration and use of dependencies smooth and well-integrated into the development cycle.

Configuring Maven in Eclipse X

Maven is a dependency management and build automation tool primarily used for Java projects. It provides a standard structure for managing project dependencies and library versions, automating the build, testing, deployment, and other processes.

Installing and Configuring Maven in Eclipse X

Eclipse X includes ready-to-use Maven integration called **M2Eclipse**, which allows you to manage Maven projects directly within the IDE. If for some reason the Maven integration is not available, you can install it from the Eclipse marketplace.

Installing M2Eclipse:

1. **Go to Menu**: In Eclipse X, click on **Help -> Eclipse Marketplace**.

2. **Search for M2Eclipse**: In the search bar, enter “Maven” or “M2Eclipse”.

3. **Install**: Click on **Install** next to **Maven Integration for Eclipse (M2Eclipse)**.

4. **Restart Eclipse X**: After installation, restart the IDE to apply the changes.

Once M2Eclipse is installed, you can manage and create Maven projects directly from Eclipse X.

Creating a Maven Project

A Maven project has a well-defined structure

and a configuration file called `pom.xml` (Project Object Model). This file contains information on how to manage the project, including external dependencies, the build lifecycle, and plugin configurations.

Steps to Create a Maven Project:

1. **New Maven Project**: Go to **File -> New -> Maven Project**.

2. **Select the Maven Archetype**: Maven archetypes are predefined project templates. You can choose the `maven-archetype-quickstart` for a simple Java project.

3. **Configure the Project**: Enter the **Group Id** (e.g., `com.my.project`), the **Artifact Id** (project name, e.g., `my-maven-project`), and the project version (e.g., `1.0-SNAPSHOT`).

4. **Generate the Project**: Eclipse X will create a preconfigured project structure, with a `src` folder for source code and a `pom.xml` file for managing dependencies.

Example `pom.xml` for a Maven Project:

```xml
<project
xmlns="http://maven.apache.org/POM/4.0.0"

xmlns:xsi="http://www.w3.org/2001/XMLSc
hema-instance"

xsi:schemaLocation="http://maven.apache.org
/POM/4.0.0
http://maven.apache.org/xsd/maven-
4.0.0.xsd">
  <modelVersion>4.0.0</modelVersion>


  <groupId>com.my.project</groupId>
  <artifactId>my-maven-project</artifactId>
  <version>1.0-SNAPSHOT</version>


  <dependencies>
    <!-- Dependency on an external library
```

```
-->
        <dependency>
    <groupId>org.springframework</groupId>
            <artifactId>spring-core</artifactId>
            <version>5.3.9</version>
        </dependency>
    </dependencies>

</project>
```

Adding a Dependency

To add a dependency in a Maven project, you simply modify the `pom.xml` file and include the desired library. For example, if you want to add a **JUnit** library for testing:

```xml
<dependencies>
   <dependency>
      <groupId>junit</groupId>
      <artifactId>junit</artifactId>
      <version>4.13.2</version>
      <scope>test</scope>
   </dependency>
</dependencies>
```

When you save the file, Eclipse X will automatically start downloading the libraries from the Maven central repository and update the project.

Using Maven Repositories

By default, Maven uses the **Maven

Central** repository to download dependencies. However, you can add other repositories, such as private or custom company repositories. To do this, you need to add the repository configuration in the `pom.xml` file:

```xml
<repositories>
    <repository>
        <id>company-repo</id>
        <url>https://repository.company.com/maven2</url>
    </repository>
</repositories>
```

Using Maven in Eclipse X

After configuring the Maven project, you can use Eclipse X to manage dependencies and build operations for the project.

Build and Test the Project:

- **Build the Project**: You can build the Maven project by going to **Run -> Run As -> Maven Build**.

- **Test**: To run tests, go to **Run -> Run As -> Maven Test**.

Useful Maven Commands in Eclipse X:

- `mvn clean`: Cleans the build files.

- `mvn compile`: Compiles the project.

- `mvn package`: Creates a package (jar or war).

- `mvn install`: Installs the package in the local Maven repository.

Complete Example: Dependency Management with Maven

Suppose you want to create a Java project with Maven that uses two dependencies: **Spring Framework** for managing inversion of control and **Log4j** for logging.

`pom.xml` Configuration with Multiple Dependencies:

```xml
<project
xmlns="http://maven.apache.org/POM/4.0.0"

xmlns:xsi="http://www.w3.org/2001/XMLSc
hema-instance"

xsi:schemaLocation="http://maven.apache.org
/POM/4.0.0
http://maven.apache.org/xsd/maven-
4.0.0.xsd">

    <modelVersion>4.0.0</modelVersion>
```

```
    <groupId>com.example.project</groupId>

    <artifactId>spring-log4j-
project</artifactId>

    <version>1.0-SNAPSHOT</version>


    <dependencies>

        <!-- Dependency on Spring Framework
-->

        <dependency>

<groupId>org.springframework</groupId>

            <artifactId>spring-context</artifactId>

            <version>5.3.9</version>

        </dependency>


        <!-- Dependency on Log4j for logging
-->

        <dependency>
```

```
<groupId>org.apache.logging.log4j</groupId>
        <artifactId>log4j-core</artifactId>
        <version>2.14.1</version>
      </dependency>
   </dependencies>
</project>
```

In this example, Maven will automatically download the **Spring** and **Log4j** dependencies, allowing you to use them in your code without worrying about manually downloading `.jar` files.

Configuring Gradle in Eclipse X

In addition to Maven, Eclipse X also supports **Gradle**, another popular dependency management and build tool. Gradle is flexible, supports both Java projects and other languages like **Groovy** and **Kotlin**, and is known for its more modern and powerful syntax compared to Maven.

Installing Gradle in Eclipse X

Eclipse X offers native integration for Gradle via the **Buildship** plugin. If it is not already installed, you can do so from the **Eclipse Marketplace**.

Steps to Install Gradle Buildship:

1. **Open the Marketplace**: Go to **Help -> Eclipse Marketplace**.

2. **Search for Buildship**: Type “Gradle” or “Buildship” in the search bar.

3. **Install Buildship**: Select **Buildship: Eclipse Plug-ins for Gradle** and click **Install**.

4. **Restart Eclipse X**: Restart the IDE to apply the changes.

Creating a Gradle Project

Once Buildship is installed, you can create new Gradle projects directly from Eclipse X.

Steps to Create a Gradle Project:

1. **New Gradle Project**: Go to **File -> New -> Gradle Project**.

2. **Configure the Project**: Provide a name for the project and specify the path.

3. **Generate the Project**: Eclipse X will create a `build.gradle` file that defines the project configurations, including dependencies.

Adding Dependencies in Gradle

The `build.gradle` file is the heart of the Gradle project, where dependencies are defined. An example of a Gradle file for a Java project using **JUnit** and **Spring

Framework** could be as follows:

```groovy
plugins {
    id 'java'
}

repositories {
    mavenCentral()
}

dependencies {
    implementation 'org.springframework:spring-context:5.3.9'
    testImplementation 'junit:junit:4.13.2'
}
```

Using Gradle in Eclipse X

Once the Gradle project is configured, you can manage dependencies and builds directly from Eclipse X. The **Gradle Tasks** window allows you to execute common commands, such as `build`, `clean`, `test`, and more.

Useful Gradle Commands:

- `gradle build`: Compiles and builds the project.

- `gradle test`: Executes the defined tests.

- `gradle clean`: Cleans the build files.

Complete Example: Gradle Configuration with Multiple Dependencies

Consider a project that uses **Gson** for JSON manipulation and **SLF4J** for logging management.

`build.gradle` File with Gson and SLF4J Dependencies:

```groovy
plugins {
    id 'java'
}

repositories {
    mavenCentral()
}

dependencies {
    implementation 'com.google.code.gson:gson:2.8.8'
    implementation 'org.slf4j:slf4j-api:1.7.32'
    implementation 'org.slf4j:slf4j-simple:1.7.32'
}
```

```

In this example, Gradle will automatically download and include the **Gson** and **SLF4J** dependencies, making them available for use in your Java project.

---

Dependency management is a fundamental part of modern development, and tools like **Maven** and **Gradle** provide great support to automate and simplify this process. **Eclipse X**, with its native integration of Maven and Gradle, offers a comprehensive and powerful development environment to manage any type of project, ensuring that dependencies are always up to date and correctly configured.

We have explored the basic concepts of dependency management, configured Maven and Gradle in Eclipse X, and provided
```

practical examples on how to add and manage external libraries in projects. By using these tools, you can develop applications more quickly and with fewer errors, fully leveraging the vast range of libraries available in the open-source community.

6.Collaboration and Version Control in Eclipse X

Effective collaboration and version control are fundamental elements in modern software development. In a team work environment, it is essential to maintain centralized management of source code, facilitate collaboration among team members, and ensure that changes are traceable and reversible. **Eclipse X** offers robust tools for managing version control through integration with systems like **Git** and **SVN** (Subversion). In this guide, we will explore:

- **Integration with Git**: How to use Git in Eclipse X to manage your code.

- **Configuring SVN**: How to set up and use Subversion in Eclipse X.

- **Team Collaboration Strategies**: Best practices for working in groups and optimizing workflow.

Integration with Git

Git is one of the most widely used version control systems in the world. It is distributed, meaning that each team member has a complete copy of the repository, making offline work and code merging simpler.

Installing and Configuring Git in Eclipse X

Eclipse X integrates Git through the **EGit** plugin, which allows you to manage Git repositories directly from the IDE interface. If you don't have EGit installed, you can add it by following these steps:

1. **Open Eclipse X**.

2. Go to **Help** -> **Eclipse Marketplace**.

3. Search for **EGit** and install the plugin.

4. Restart Eclipse X.

Creating a New Git Repository

After configuring EGit, you can create a new Git repository:

1. **Create a New Project**: Go to **File** -> **New** -> **Project** and choose the desired project type.

2. **Initialize the Repository**: Right-click on the project in the **Package Explorer** view, select **Team** -> **Initialize Git Repository**.

3. **Add Files to the Repository**: After initializing the repository, you can add files. Right-click on the file or folder and select **Team** -> **Add to Staging Area**.

Performing Common Git Operations

EGit provides a graphical interface for performing common Git operations. Some of the most frequent include:

- **Commit**: To save changes to the local repository.

  1. Right-click on the project and select **Team** -> **Commit**.

  2. Write a commit message and select the files to include.

  3. Click **Commit**.

- **Push**: To send changes to the remote repository.

  1. Select **Team** -> **Push to Upstream** to send changes to the remote server.

- **Pull**: To download the latest changes from the remote repository.

  1. Right-click on the project and select

Team -> **Pull**.

Branch Management

Branches are essential for working on different features without disrupting the main work. With EGit, you can easily create and manage branches:

- **Create a New Branch**:

  1. Select **Team** -> **Switch to Another Branch**.

  2. Click on **New** to create a new branch, name it, and confirm.

- **Merge a Branch**:

  1. Switch to the main branch (e.g., `main` or `master`).

  2. Select **Team** -> **Merge** and choose the branch to merge.

Practical Example of Collaboration with Git

Imagine working in a team on a web development project. Each developer can create their own branch to work on specific features, such as a new login page.

1. Each team member creates a branch for their feature (e.g., `feature/login-page`).

2. Once the feature is complete, the developer commits the changes and pushes them to the remote repository.

3. Other team members can then pull the changes and test the new features.

4. When all features are ready, the team can merge them into the main branch.

Configuring SVN

SVN is a centralized version control

system, often used in larger companies and projects. Unlike Git, where each developer has a complete copy of the repository, with SVN, the code is stored in a central repository.

Installing SVN in Eclipse X

Eclipse X supports SVN through the **Subclipse** plugin. Follow these steps to install it:

1. **Open Eclipse X**.

2. Go to **Help** -> **Eclipse Marketplace**.

3. Search for **Subclipse** and install the plugin.

4. Restart Eclipse X.

Configuring an SVN Repository

After installing Subclipse, you can configure a new project to use SVN:

1. **Create a New Project**: As with Git, start by creating a new project.

2. **Add the Project to SVN**: Right-click on the project and select **Team** -> **Connect to SVN**.

3. **Set the Repository URL**: Enter the URL of the SVN repository and confirm.

Common SVN Operations

Subclipse also offers a graphical interface to manage common SVN operations. Here are some of the most used:

- **Update the Project**: To download the latest changes from the repository.

  1. Right-click on the project and select **Team** -> **Update**.

- **Commit Changes**: To send changes to the central repository.

  1. Select **Team** -> **Commit**.

  2. Add a commit message and select the files to include.

  3. Click **OK**.

- **Conflict Resolution**: If there are conflicts between your changes and others, Subclipse will notify you and allow you to resolve them through the interface.

Practical Example of Collaboration with SVN

In a team using SVN, the workflow might look like this:

1. Each team member regularly updates their local project to get the latest changes.

2. When a developer completes a feature, they

commit their changes to the central repository.

3. Other team members receive the update and can test the new feature.

4. If there are conflicts, they can resolve them using the Subclipse interface.

Team Collaboration Strategies

Effective collaboration within a team is critical for a project's success. Here are some strategies that can help optimize workflow:

1. Define a Clear Workflow

Establish a clear and shared workflow among team members. For example, you can follow the **Git Flow** model, which involves using branches for different phases of the project lifecycle, such as development, testing, and production.

2. Use Pull Requests

If you use Git, **pull requests** are a great way to review proposed changes before they are merged into the main branch. This allows other team members to examine the code and provide feedback.

3. Conduct Code Reviews

Encourage code reviews to improve code quality and share knowledge within the team. You can set up a formal review process using tools integrated into Eclipse X or external services like GitHub or Bitbucket.

4. Document Changes

Ensure that each commit contains clear and meaningful messages. This helps other team members understand the changes made and why they were made.

5. Use Feature Branches

Using feature branches for each new functionality allows you to isolate development work, reducing the risk of conflicts and facilitating dependency management among features.

6. Schedule Regular Meetings

Plan regular meetings to discuss project progress, address issues, and plan future work. These meetings can be weekly or biweekly, depending on the size of the project and the team.

7. Manage Dependencies Efficiently

Use tools like Maven or Gradle to manage dependencies. This ensures that all team members use the same versions of libraries, reducing the risk of compatibility issues.

Collaboration and version control are essential for effective teamwork in software development. With **Eclipse X**, you can leverage native integration with Git and SVN to manage your code easily and intuitively. Following best practices for version control and implementing clear collaboration strategies will help ensure your team works synergistically, producing high-quality software efficiently.

7.Testing and Code Quality in Eclipse X

Code quality and validation are fundamental to software development. In **Eclipse X**, developers have access to a range of tools and techniques to ensure their code is effectively tested and meets quality standards. This guide will explore various aspects of code quality, including best practices for writing unit tests, using code analysis tools, and integrating with testing frameworks.

Writing Unit Tests

Unit tests are tests that verify the functionality of a single unit of code, such as a function or method. Writing unit tests is essential to ensure that the code works as intended and to prevent regressions in the future.

1. Setting Up the Testing Environment

To start writing unit tests in Eclipse X, you can use a testing framework like **JUnit**. JUnit is one of the most popular testing frameworks for Java and comes with many features to facilitate the writing and execution of tests.

Installing JUnit

1. **Create a New Java Project**: In Eclipse X, go to **File** -> **New** -> **Java Project**.

2. **Add JUnit**: You can add JUnit as a dependency in your `pom.xml` file if you're using Maven. Here's an example:

```xml
<dependency>
    <groupId>junit</groupId>
    <artifactId>junit</artifactId>
    <version>4.13.2</version>
    <scope>test</scope>
```

```
    </dependency>
```

2. Writing a Unit Test

Once JUnit is set up, you can start writing unit tests. Here’s an example of a simple test for a class that calculates the sum of two numbers.

Class to Test

```java
public class Calculator {
    public int add(int a, int b) {
        return a + b;
    }
}
```

Unit Test

```java
import static org.junit.Assert.assertEquals;
import org.junit.Test;

public class CalculatorTest {
    @Test
    public void testAdd() {
        Calculator calculator = new Calculator();
        assertEquals(5, calculator.add(2, 3));
        assertEquals(0, calculator.add(-1, 1));
        assertEquals(-2, calculator.add(-1, -1));
    }
}
```

3. Running the Tests

To run unit tests in Eclipse X:

1. Right-click on the test file in the **Package Explorer** view.

2. Select **Run As** -> **JUnit Test**.

Eclipse X will show the results of the tests in a new view, highlighting passed and failed tests.

4. Writing Parameterized Tests

JUnit also allows you to write parameterized tests, meaning you can run the same test with different inputs. This is useful for testing various scenarios without duplicating code.

Example of a Parameterized Test

```java
import static org.junit.Assert.assertEquals;
import org.junit.Test;
import org.junit.runner.RunWith;
import org.junit.runners.Parameterized;

@RunWith(Parameterized.class)
public class CalculatorParameterizedTest {
    private int a;
    private int b;
    private int expected;

    public CalculatorParameterizedTest(int a, int b, int expected) {
        this.a = a;
        this.b = b;
        this.expected = expected;
    }
```

```
    @Parameterized.Parameters
    public static Object[][] data() {
        return new Object[][] {
            { 2, 3, 5 },
            { -1, 1, 0 },
            { -1, -1, -2 }
        };
    }

    @Test
    public void testAdd() {
        Calculator calculator = new Calculator();
        assertEquals(expected, calculator.add(a, b));
    }
}
```

Using Code Analysis Tools

Static code analysis is an effective way to improve code quality and identify issues before they become bugs. Eclipse X offers built-in analysis tools that can help you maintain high standards in your code.

1. SonarLint

SonarLint is a code analysis tool that integrates well with Eclipse X. It provides real-time feedback on code issues while you write.

Installing SonarLint

1. Go to **Help** -> **Eclipse Marketplace**.

2. Search for **SonarLint** and install the plugin.

3. Restart Eclipse X.

Using SonarLint

After installing SonarLint, you can use it to analyze your code:

1. Right-click on a file or folder in your project.

2. Select **Analyze** -> **Analyze with SonarLint**.

3. SonarLint will highlight issues such as vulnerabilities, bugs, and code smells directly in the editor.

2. Checkstyle

Checkstyle is another useful tool that helps ensure code follows specific style standards. You can configure it to check formatting, complexity, and more.

Installing Checkstyle

1. Go to **Help** -> **Eclipse Marketplace**.

2. Search for **Checkstyle** and install the plugin.

3. Restart Eclipse X.

Configuring Checkstyle

You can configure Checkstyle to use a specific configuration file. Here’s how:

1. Go to **Window** -> **Preferences**.

2. Select **Checkstyle** and add a new configuration file.

3. Choose your custom `checkstyle.xml` file or use a default one.

Integrating with Testing Frameworks

In addition to JUnit, you can integrate other testing frameworks like **Mockito** to test the behavior of objects in isolation.

1. Using Mockito for Testing

Mockito is a mocking framework that allows you to simulate the behavior of objects to test code units in isolation.

Adding Mockito to the Project

If you're using Maven, you can add Mockito as a dependency in your `pom.xml`:

```xml
<dependency>
    <groupId>org.mockito</groupId>
    <artifactId>mockito-core</artifactId>
    <version>3.11.2</version>
```

```
    <scope>test</scope>
</dependency>
```

Example of Testing with Mockito

Imagine you have a `UserService` class that depends on a repository to access user data. You can use Mockito to mock this repository in your tests.

Class to Test

```java
public class UserService {
    private UserRepository userRepository;

    public UserService(UserRepository userRepository) {
```

```
        this.userRepository = userRepository;
    }

    public User getUserById(int id) {
        return userRepository.findById(id);
    }
}
```

Test with Mockito

```java
import static org.mockito.Mockito.*;
import static org.junit.Assert.*;
import org.junit.Test;

public class UserServiceTest {
    @Test
```

```
    public void testGetUserById() {
        UserRepository mockRepository =
mock(UserRepository.class);
        UserService userService = new
UserService(mockRepository);

        User mockUser = new User(1, "John
Doe");

when(mockRepository.findById(1)).thenRetur
n(mockUser);

        User result =
userService.getUserById(1);
        assertEquals("John Doe",
result.getName());
    }
}
```

Optimizing Performance

Improving Eclipse X Performance

The performance of Eclipse X can affect your productivity. Here are some tips to enhance your user experience.

1. **Increase Allocated Memory**: You can increase the memory available to Eclipse by modifying the `eclipse.ini` file. Add or modify the following lines:

```
-Xms256m

-Xmx2048m
```

2. **Disable Unused Plugins**: If you have plugins that you don’t use, disable them to improve performance. Go to **Help** -> **About Eclipse** -> **Installation Details**

and disable unnecessary plugins.

3. **Optimize Views**: You can hide views and perspectives that you don’t use frequently to reduce memory load.

Troubleshooting Common Performance Issues

Common performance issues may include:

- **Slow Startup**: If Eclipse takes a long time to start, check the memory configuration and reduce unnecessary plugins.

- **Editor Response Delays**: If the editor is slow to respond, try disabling features like auto-completion or real-time analysis.

Troubleshooting

Common Errors and Resolutions

1. **Class Not Found**: If Eclipse can't find a class, make sure the file is present in the build path and that the project is configured correctly.

2. **Compilation Errors**: Check the error messages in the **Problems** view. Often, syntax or import errors can cause compilation issues.

3. **Eclipse Freezes**: If Eclipse frequently freezes, consider increasing allocated memory and disabling unused plugins.

Frequently Asked Questions

1. **What is the difference between JUnit and TestNG?**

JUnit is a testing framework primarily focused on unit testing, while TestNG offers more advanced features for more complex tests and support for parallel execution.

2. **Can I run unit tests without a testing framework?**

While it's possible to write tests without a framework, using one like JUnit or TestNG greatly simplifies writing, executing, and managing tests.

3. **How can I improve test coverage in my project?**

Use tools like **JaCoCo** to analyze test coverage and identify areas of your code that need additional tests.

4. **What should I do if a test fails?**

Start by analyzing the error message and context of the test. Use the debugger to examine the execution flow and identify the root cause of the failure.

Code quality is essential for successful software development. **Eclipse X** provides a wide range of tools for testing your code, analyzing its quality, and optimizing performance. By implementing unit tests, using code analysis tools, and following best development practices, you can ensure that your software is robust, maintainable, and ready to face future challenges. Knowing how to

troubleshoot common issues and optimize Eclipse X performance will help you become a more efficient and productive developer.

8.Glossary of Eclipse X

The glossary of Eclipse X is an important reference tool that provides a comprehensive understanding of the terms and features most commonly used within the integrated development environment (IDE). This glossary is designed to assist both beginners and experienced developers in effectively navigating the various components of Eclipse X. Below is a detailed list of terms with descriptions, examples, and usage contexts.

A

API (Application Programming Interface)

An API is a set of rules and tools that allows programmers to interact with software. In Eclipse X, APIs can be used to develop plugins or extensions that enhance the functionality of the IDE.

Example: Using the Eclipse API, a

developer can create a plugin that adds new refactoring features.

AST (Abstract Syntax Tree)

An abstract syntax tree is a hierarchical representation of the syntax of a program. Eclipse X uses AST to analyze source code and provide assistance tools, such as autocompletion and refactoring.

Example: When writing code in Java, Eclipse generates an AST that represents expressions, statements, and code blocks.

B

Build

The term "build" refers to the process of compiling source code into an executable format. In Eclipse X, you can manage the build process through project configuration options.

Example: After making changes to the code, perform a "build" to generate the JAR file for your project.

Branch

A branch is a separate version of the source code in a version control system. Eclipse X supports branch management, allowing developers to work on different features without interfering with the main code.

Example: A development team creates a branch called `feature/login` to work on a new login feature.

C

Compiler

The compiler is a program that translates source code written in a programming language (such as Java) into bytecode or executable machine code. Eclipse X includes a built-in compiler for Java.

Example: When you compile your project, the Eclipse compiler translates the source code into Java bytecode, ready to be executed on the Java Virtual Machine (JVM).

Debugging

Debugging is the process of identifying and resolving bugs or errors in the code. Eclipse X offers built-in debugging tools to facilitate this process.

Example: Using the Eclipse debugger, you can set breakpoints in your code and analyze the execution flow step by step.

Dependency Management

Dependency management refers to the management of libraries and packages that a project uses. In Eclipse X, you can use tools like Maven or Gradle to manage dependencies.

Example: Add an external library to your project by modifying the Maven `pom.xml` file.

D

Deployment

Deployment is the process of distributing an application in a production environment. In Eclipse X, you can configure your project for deployment on various servers or platforms.

Example: After testing your application, you deploy it on a web server using Eclipse's deployment configurations.

DSL (Domain-Specific Language)

A domain-specific language is a programming language designed for a specific application area. Eclipse X supports the creation and editing of DSLs through modeling tools.

Example: You can use Eclipse to develop a DSL for defining business rules.

E

Editor

The editor is the part of the IDE where you write your code. Eclipse X offers an advanced editor with features like autocompletion, syntax highlighting, and refactoring.

Example: The Eclipse editor automatically suggests keywords while you write Java code.

Environment

The development environment is the set of tools and configurations necessary for software development. Eclipse X provides a highly configurable environment for various programming languages.

Example: You can configure Eclipse to develop Java, Python, or C++ applications based on your needs.

F

Framework

A framework is a support structure for application development. Eclipse X integrates with various frameworks, such as Spring and Hibernate, to simplify Java application development.

Example: You can use the Spring framework to develop web applications and manage project configuration directly from Eclipse.

Git

Git is a distributed version control system that allows tracking changes in source code. Eclipse X offers robust integration with Git through the EGit plugin.

Example: You can use EGit to perform Git operations like commit, push, and pull directly from the IDE.

I

IDE (Integrated Development Environment)

An IDE is a software application that provides comprehensive tools for software development. Eclipse X is an open-source IDE designed to support various programming languages.

Example: Using Eclipse as an IDE, you have access to a code editor, a compiler, and debugging tools all in one interface.

Import

Importing refers to the process of adding an existing project or external libraries to your development environment. Eclipse X supports various import modes.

Example: You can import an existing Maven project into Eclipse using the **Import** option from the menu.

L

Library

A library is a collection of precompiled code that you can use in your projects. Eclipse X allows you to easily add external libraries to your project.

Example: You can add the Apache Commons library to simplify common operations in your code.

Logger

A logger is a tool that allows recording events and messages during application execution. Eclipse X supports various logging libraries, such as Log4j and SLF4J.

Example: Using Log4j, you can log debug messages and information about your application's operations.

M

Maven

Maven is a dependency management and build system for Java projects. In Eclipse X, you can configure Maven to manage libraries and the project lifecycle.

Example: You can define dependencies in the `pom.xml` file, and Maven will automatically manage the download of the required libraries.

Plugin

A plugin is a software component that adds functionality to an existing application. Eclipse X is highly extensible and supports a wide range of plugins for various purposes.

Example: You can install a plugin for support of additional programming languages, such as Python or Ruby.

R

Refactoring

Refactoring is the process of modifying

existing code to improve its structure without changing its external behavior. Eclipse X offers tools to facilitate refactoring.

Example: You can rename a variable, and Eclipse will automatically update all occurrences in the code.

Repository

A repository is a place where the source code is stored and managed. It can be a local repository on your computer or a remote repository on platforms like GitHub.

Example: You can clone a remote Git repository to start working on an existing project.

S

SDK (Software Development Kit)

An SDK is a set of development tools that allows you to create applications for a specific platform. Eclipse X supports various SDKs for software development.

Example: You can download and configure the Java SDK to develop Java applications in Eclipse.

Syntax Highlighting

Syntax highlighting is an editor feature that displays source code in different colors based on the type of element (keywords, comments, strings, etc.). This feature facilitates reading and writing code.

Example: When writing a Java class, keywords like `public` and `class` are highlighted in blue to distinguish them from variable names.

T

Unit Test

A unit test is a test that verifies the functionality of a single unit of code. In Eclipse X, you can use frameworks like JUnit to write and run unit tests.

Example: Write unit tests for your `Calculator` class to ensure that the addition and subtraction methods work correctly.

Version Control

Version control is the process of managing changes to source code over time. Eclipse X integrates version control tools, such as Git and SVN, to facilitate collaboration among developers.

Example: Using Git, you can track changes made to the code, revert to previous versions, and collaborate with other team members.

U

Unit Testing

Unit testing is a development practice that involves writing tests for individual units of code. This practice helps ensure that the code works as expected and prevents regressions.

Example: Write unit tests for your sum function to ensure it handles edge cases correctly, such as negative numbers and zero.

UML (Unified Modeling Language)

UML is a modeling language used to specify, visualize, construct, and document the components of a software system. Eclipse X offers tools for creating UML diagrams.

Example: You can use Eclipse to create a UML class diagram that represents the structure of your project.

The Eclipse X glossary provides a useful knowledge base for understanding the various features and terms used within the IDE. Familiarizing yourself with these terms will not only enhance your ability to use Eclipse X but also help you communicate more effectively with other developers and better understand the software development process. Whether you're a beginner or an expert, having a solid understanding of these concepts is essential for success in the world of software development.

Index

www.ingramcontent.com/pod-product-compliance
Lightning Source LLC
Chambersburg PA
CBHW050258230526
45471CB00005B/1933

* 9 7 9 8 3 3 9 8 7 5 0 3 1 *